11-24
STRAND PRICE
$ 5.00

FOR BILL.
NATURALLY, WHO IS EVERY PART OF MY LIFE AND MY LOVE,
AND WHO FINDS THE WAY TO MAKE ALL THINGS POSSIBLE.

ROMEO & JULIET
THE LOVE STORY IN DANCE

BY NANCY ELLISON

A PHOTOGRAPHIC BALLET IN FIVE ACTS, STARRING PALOMA HERRERA AND ANGEL CORELLA
INTRODUCTION BY KEVIN McKENZIE, BALLET LIBRETTO NOTES AND CONTINUITY BY AMY EPHRON

UNIVERSE

ACKNOWLEDGMENTS

Many helped our project significantly: Giuseppe Cipriani, who with one phone call made it happen; Stefania Rattin, who answered Giuseppe's call; Michael Kaiser, for his love and counsel; Kevin McKenzie, for his spirit and support; David Richardson, for his creative eye; Amy Ephron, for her generosity of spirit; doll maker Giulia Vanni; La Maison Moderne, New York; Mallory Hathaway; Aldo Werdin and the Due Torri Hotel Baglioni; Paolo Valerio (our Veronese Tybalt), who lent us his roof and costumes and gave us his friendship and good humor; my agent Tom Wallace; the talented team at Universe/Rizzoli: Marco Pittini, Antonio Polito, Charles Miers, Elizabeth White, and Robin Key; graphic designers Trey Laird and Christopher Twele; my editor, Sandy Gilbert; and to Paloma and Angel for being, not only consummate artists, but wonderfully good sports as well.

Finally, I would like to thank an unknown security guard at the Milan airport who secretly reduced the level of damage inflicted on my exposed film which was forced through X-ray by the airport police. Bless him!

FIRST PUBLISHED IN THE UNITED STATES OF AMERICA IN 1998
BY UNIVERSE PUBLISHING, A DIVISION OF RIZZOLI INTERNATIONAL PUBLICATIONS, INC.
300 PARK AVENUE SOUTH, NEW YORK, NY 10010

COPYRIGHT © 1998 UNIVERSE PUBLISHING
PHOTOGRAPHY COPYRIGHT © 1998 NANCY ELLISON

ALL RIGHTS RESERVED. NO PART OF THIS PUBLICATION MAY BE REPRODUCED, STORED IN A RETRIEVAL SYSTEM, OR TRANSMITTED IN ANY FORM OR BY ANY MEANS, ELECTRONIC, MECHANICAL, PHOTOCOPYING, RECORDING, OR OTHERWISE, WITHOUT PRIOR CONSENT OF THE PUBLISHERS.

LIBRARY OF CONGRESS CATALOG CARD NUMBER: 98-61127
98 99 00 01 02/10 9 8 7 6 5 4 3 2 1

DESIGN AND TYPOGRAPHY BY TREY LAIRD AND CHRISTOPHER TWELE
PRINTED IN SINGAPORE

PREFACE
by Nancy Ellison

PHOTOGRAPHING SHAKESPEARE'S VERONA

Everybody knows the love story of Juliet and her Romeo. Who has not identified with those two characters, rooted for their love, and been moved by their tragic fate? It was a surprise to me, therefore, that while researching *Romeo and Juliet* for this book, I was unable to find any visual representations, except for poet William Blake's, in my art history library. I could not believe a story so eternally fresh and compelling had not excited painters. The characters are young, beautiful, and in the throes of passion. The themes are at once simple and profound.

Composers, however, have found *Romeo and Juliet* a fertile source of inspiration. Tchaikovsky, Prokofiev, Berlioz, Bernstein (*West Side Story*), and Delius have all produced operas or ballets based on Shakespeare's play. Sergei Prokofiev's *Romeo and Juliet* score, alone, has been the framework for ballets choreographed by

Leonid Lavrovsky, Frederick Ashton, John Cranko, and Kenneth MacMillian. It is the American Ballet Theatre's production of the MacMillian ballet, which entered the company's repertory in 1985, that has been an inspiration to me. This book represents a personal visual interpretation done in collaboration with ABT's principal dancers Paloma Herrera and Angel Corella. The plot sequence remains the same as the play and the ballet, but some acts have been collapsed, and some scenes moved to different locations.

Romeo, a bello, Veronese lad, lost in unrequited love, is rescued through love-at-first-sight by a daughter of the sworn enemy. A midnight rendezvous leads to elopement and two months of passionate trysts; *two months* of Romeo climbing onto the balcony of Juliet's bedroom before her cousin Tybalt's fateful murder. Not in *our* story, but in Arthur Brooke's *Tragical History of Romeus and Juliet*, printed in 1562 (at least thirty years before Shakespeare's tragedy), Romeus does indeed have two months of passion with his Juliet before their young lives fall apart. Shakespeare took Brooke's simpler plot line and condensed the time sequence to a more highly dramatic five days — which is exactly the time I had to photograph our dance version of the story.

We shot on location in "fair" Verona itself, where, of course, Shakespeare sets his play. Verona, with its beautiful medieval and renaissance architecture, offered us genuine and inspiring stage sets. With Paloma Herrera and Angel Corella reenacting their roles as Romeo and Juliet we began one cold rainy day at the picturesque Scala della Ragione (the Staircase of Reason) where the opening sequence of the ballet took place. Shakespeare's Romeo and Juliet experience their most private and romantic moments at night, when they are alone together: the ball, the balcony and courtyard pas de deux, and the wedding night in Juliet's chamber. The most crucial of these scenes, the balcony pas de deux, is outdoors, allowing us the opportunity to photograph "day-for-night" (a cinematic technique used to create the effect of night during daylight). The barracks-side courtyard of the Castelvecchio was chosen for its spacious façade. Unable to use any church locations for the elopement or tomb scenes, we were forced to chase the sun through the downtown

streets of Verona trying to find a similar numinous light and ambiance. After being evicted from an underground Roman ruin where we were shooting the tomb finale, I had Juliet and her Romeo playing dead in various locations around the Piazza dei Signori. Ultimately, we found a site that gave Juliet a proper marble slab for her final pose and light and atmosphere to match the beginning of the scene. The Due Torri Hotel Baglioni, with its decorative Venetian interiors, became the setting for the Capulets' ball. Naturally, the close-ups of Juliet's balcony scene were photographed at the so-called "Juliet's Balcony," in the tiny courtyard off the Via Cappello, which is never without its hundreds of curious tourists crowding the cramped space.

With the exception of the rainy day at the Old Marketplace Courtyard shooting around the Scala della Ragione, the fall weather was clear and beautiful and warm enough for the dancers.

LOVE AMONG THE CODO DUELLO

Why is it that in all the love stories that grip our hearts the most, the characters usually die, one or both, in each other's arms? Is it simply that the throes of passion are too intense to survive, or are there other elements that drive these tales to their inevitable, tragic conclusion? In fairy tales such as *Sleeping Beauty* or *Cinderella*, the endings are happily-ever-after. They are, after all, a form of wish fulfillment. Children, especially, need to hear that dreams can come true, that everything in life is fair, that good overcomes bad, and that it is safe to go to bed at night and expect to awaken intact the next morning.

Not so in tales of tragedy. Unwittingly, artists become co-conspirators with the community to protect its social fabric from any action that violates that order. It is more than just star-crossed destiny that delivers Romeo and Juliet to their woeful finale. Long-standing social laws are overturned by the lovers. In early Verona's intolerant and reckless "codo duello" society, where the dueling code of prideful machismo prevailed, "honour" commanded over reason. In *The Shakespearean Metaphor* (London, 1978) Ralph Berry writes, "What we have in *Romeo and Juliet* is a complete social context for an action, a society that is unable to cope with consequences of its own deficiencies."

In not respecting the appropriate enmity between feuding clans, Shakespeare's lovers defy both familial pressure and the community's conventional behavior. It fascinates me that Friar Lawrence (representing the Church, ergo God) sides with the disobedient lovers rather than with their families — a reflection of the still lingering belief at the time that society is secular and therefore inherently evil. "God is Love," but, alas, that love must be eternal to survive. Sacrifice, suffering, loss, and death is the only transcendent path.

Centuries before, Dante Alighieri wrote, *Amor condusse noi ad una morte*. "Love led us to one death."

THE LOVE STORY IN DANCE
by Kevin McKenzie

For many people, the word "ballet" conjures up images of swans, wilis, and sylphs — lines of ballerinas in white tulle moving in unison. And, indeed, *Swan Lake, Giselle,* and the other classical "tutu" ballets can transport you into another world.

Yet to me, *Romeo and Juliet* is the perfect story ballet. Suffused with drama, humor, beauty, and violence, *Romeo and Juliet* is populated by real people feeling honest emotions and facing true life problems. One doesn't have to believe in evil sorcerers, women turned into swans, or avenging spirits to experience *Romeo and Juliet.* Not surprisingly, *Romeo and Juliet* is the most modern of the major story ballets. While the story takes place some five hundred years ago, the ballet of *Romeo and Juliet* was choreographed to twentieth-century music and appeals to contemporary sensibilities.

When I danced Romeo, I believed in who I was and what I was doing. I always felt more connected to Romeo than to the other characters I portrayed. Romeo's range of emotions were familiar to me — the excitement of meeting a beautiful girl, the joys of courtship, and the fear of loss. The challenge was to portray these emotions honestly while dancing the steps created by the choreographer.

Now, as an artistic director with responsibility for staging these ballets, I realize that *Romeo and Juliet* "works" as a ballet for other reasons. *Romeo and Juliet* is, above all, a story of youth — and ballet dancers are so young. While many dance lovers think fondly of the last performances of Margot Fonteyn, Natalia Makarova, and other immortal ballerinas as Juliet, I am thrilled by the first performances of those ballerinas I have coached in the role — Ashley Tuttle, Yan Chen, and, yes, Paloma Herrera.

Equally moving to me are the Romeos created by young men searching to capture a wide range of emotions in movement. This role challenged me throughout my career. How gratifying it is to help other young men, including Angel Corella, tackle this role for the first time. And, my, how difficult this ballet is to perform. The challenge in every story ballet, of course, is to make the vast technical challenges appear effortless to the audience — they must believe that every dancer's movements flow from their emotional cores. But the realism of *Romeo and Juliet* places additional demands on dancers to appear as teenagers, not important dancers. The "star power" that can add to one's enjoyment of the grand pas de deux from *Sleeping Beauty* or *Don Quixote* can ruin a performance of *Romeo and Juliet*.

The audience must believe the performers. This is the story of teenagers — anxious and emotional and fully expecting that around every corner life holds a magic delight. We must feel this as the ballet begins. We must experience Romeo's first sight of Juliet at the ball. We must appreciate her shyness, her incipient maturity, and her growing sense of helplessness. I would dare say that these central moments work better for me when performed by vital, youthful dancers than by actors trying to perfect Shakespearean line readings.

But I am certainly not going to suggest that Shakespeare's plays are anything less than works of genius. In fact, Shakespeare achieved a rare feat: he created a story that can be told entirely in pictures. This is the requirement of any great story ballet and is the principal reason *Romeo and Juliet* has become one of the most popular of its genre. I cannot imagine a similar ballet of *Hamlet*, for example. The complexity of the characters in *Hamlet* emerges from language, not pictures.

This pictorial quality, not surprisingly, challenges Nancy Ellison. Her photographs tell the story of *Romeo and Juliet* clearly, concisely, and with deep emotion. (A luxury enjoyed by a photographer but not afforded a choreographer is the ability to bring dancers to the original locations in Verona where Romeo and Juliet lived and died.) It is a treat to have at our fingertips the work of such a magnificent group of artists: Nancy Ellison, Paloma Herrera, Angel Corella, and, yes, William Shakespeare.

CAST

ROMEO, SON OF THE MOUNTAGUES
ANGEL CORELLA

JULIET, DAUGHTER OF THE CAPULETS
PALOMA HERRERA

MERCUTIO, FRIEND TO ROMEO
PARIS, A YOUNG COUNT AND SUITOR TO JULIET
CLINTON LUCKETT

TYBALT, NEPHEW TO CAPULET'S WIFE
PAOLO VALERIO

ESCALUS, PRINCE OF VERONA
DAVID RICHARDSON

NURSE TO JULIET
PIA SHERIDAN

FRIAR LAWRENCE, FRANCISCAN CONFESSOR TO ROMEO AND JULIET
WILLIAM ROLLNICK

CREW — Producer, WILLIAM ROLLNICK • Production Manager, STEFANIA RATTIN • Choreographer, DAVID RICHARDSON • First Assistant, JULIAN KAISER • Second Assistant, STEFANO SACCMANI • Costumes and Styling, PIA SHERIDAN • Styling, PAULA FOX • Make-up, IRENE CAVALLI

PROLOGUE

Two Households both alike in Dignity,
In fair Verona, where we lay our Scene,
From auncient Grudge break to new Mutiny,
Where Civil Blood makes Civil Hands unclean;
From forth the fatal Loins of these two Foes
A pair of Star-cross'd Lovers take their Life,
Whose misadventur'd piteous Overthrows
Doth with their Death bury their Parents' Strife.
The fearful Passage of their Death-mark'd Love,
And the Continuance of their Parents' Rage,
Which but their Children's End nought could remove,
Is now the Two Hours' Traffic of our Stage,
The which, if you with patient Ears attend,
What heare shall miss, our Toil shall strive to mend.

ACT I

EARLY MORNING AND THE MARKET IN VERONA IS STILL EMPTY AS THE LIGHTS COME UP AND THE STAGE IS SET AT THE MARKETPLACE, BY THE SCALA DELLA RAGIONE (THE STAIRCASE OF REASON) ... AND THE BALLET SEQUENCES BEGIN.

AS ROMEO AND MERCUTIO, FROM THE FAMILY OF MOUNTAGUE, LINGER UNDER THE STAIRS, TYBALT, A NEPHEW OF CAPULET, APPEARS BEHIND A PILLAR, A FEW FEET AWAY, AND STANDS THERE QUIETLY, AS IF WAITING FOR HIS MOMENT.

OF COURSE, A FIGHT ENSUES BETWEEN THE CAPULETS AND MOUNTAGUES, AS TYBALT DRAWS HIS SWORD.

TYBALT
Turn thee, look upon thy Death.
What, drawn and talk of Peace? I hate the word
As I hate Hell, all Mountagues, and thee:
Have at thee, Coward.

THE PRINCE OF VERONA, TIRED OF THE FAMILIES' ENDLESS FIGHTING, APPEARS AT THE TOP OF THE STAIRS AND DECREES THAT WHO NEXT OF THE CAPULETS AND MOUNTAGUES SHALL FIGHT, SHALL PAY FOR IT WITH THEIR LIFE.

PRINCE
Rebellious Subjects, Enemies to Peace,
Profaners of this Neighbour-stained Steel.
— Will they not hear? — What ho, you Men, you Beasts,
That quench the Fire of your pernicious Rage
With purple Fountains issuing from your Veins
On pain of Torture, from those Bloody Hands
Throw your mistempered Weapons to the Ground
And hear the Sentence of your moved Prince. . . .
If ever you disturb our Streets again,
Your Lives shall pay the Forfeit of the Peace.

ROMEO

Here's much to do with Hate, but more with Love.
Why then, O brawling Love, O loving Hate,
O any thing of Nothing first create.
O heavy Lightness, serious Vanity,
Misshapen Chaos of well-seeming Forms!
Feather of Lead, bright Smoke, cold Fire, sick Health;
Still waking Sleep, that is not what it is.
This Love feel I, that feel no Love in this.
Doest thou not laugh? . . .
Why, such is Love's Transgression.
Griefs of mine own lie heavy in my Breast,
Which thou wilt propagate to have it prest
With more of thine. This Love that thou hast shown
Doth add more Grief to too much of mine own.
Love is a Smoke made with the Fume of Sighs;
Being purg'd, a Fire sparkling in Lovers' Eyes;
Being vex'd, a Sea nourish'd with Loving Tears.
What is it else? A Madness most discreet,
A choking Gall, and a preserving Sweet.
Farewell, my Coze.

Romeo, who as the ballet has opened, has had his advances to the lovely Rosalie spurned, muses about the state of his heart. To which, in the original text, he has asked his cousin Benvolio, "O, teach me how I should forget to think . . ." And Benvolio has replied, "By giving liberty unto thine eyes. Examine other beauties."

IN THE BALLET, AS JULIET IS AT PLAY WITH HER NURSE, HER NURSE'S ARM BRUSHES HER BREAST AND SHE REALIZES JULIET, HER CHARGE, IS NO LONGER A CHILD . . .

NURSE
Now by my Maidenhead, at twelve year old
I bad her come. — What, Lamb? What, Ladybird?
— God forbid, where's this Girl? — What, Juliet? . . .
Thou wast the prettiest Babe that e'er I nurs'd.
And I might live to see thee married once,
I have my Wish. . . .

JULIET
It is an Hour that I dream not of.

ROMEO, MERCUTIO, AND BENVOLIO, DISGUISED IN MASKS, IN A MOMENT OF CAPRICIOUSNESS, AND AWARE THAT THEY ARE COURTING DANGER, HAVE STOLEN INTO THE CAPULETS' BALL. AS ROMEO IS HIDING IN PLAIN SIGHT, DELIGHTING IN HIS MISCHIEF, HE CATCHES HIS FIRST GLANCE OF JULIET, WHO IS DANCING WITH PARIS.

and then she seems to be dancing for him . . .

ROMEO
What Lady's that which doth enrich the Hand
Of yonder Knight? . . .
O she doth teach the Torches to burn bright.
It seems she hangs upon the Cheek of Night
As a rich Jewel in an Ethiop's Ear:
Beauty too rich for Use, for Earth too dear.
So shows a snowy Dove trooping with Crows
As yonder Lady o'er her Fellows shows.
The Measure done, I'll watch her place of Stand,
And, touching hers, make blessed my rude Hand.
Did my Heart love till now? Forswear it, Sight;
For I ne'er saw true Beauty till this Night.

Unaware that they each dance with their family's sworn enemy, they dance together and, in the purity of that moment, recognize their own true love.... And, innocent of the fact that they are being observed by Tybalt, who recognizes Romeo's voice and realizes that Juliet is in the arms of a Mountague.

TYBALT
This by his Voice should be a Mountague. Fetch me my Rapier, Boy.

ROMEO

If I profane with my unworthiest Hand
This holy Shrine, the gentle Sin in this:
My Lips, two blushing Pilgrims, ready stand
To smooth that rough Touch with a tender Kiss.

JULIET

Good Pilgrim, you do wrong your Hand too much,
Which mannerly Devotion shows in this,
For Saints have Hands that Pilgrims' Hands do touch,
And Palm to Palm is holy Palmers' Kiss.

ROMEO

Have not Saints Lips, and holy Palmers too?

JULIET

I, Pilgrim: Lips that they must use in Pray'r.

ROMEO

O then, dear Saint, let Lips do what Hands do:
They pray. Grant thou, lest Faith turn to Despair.

NURSE

His Name is Romeo, and a Mountague:
The onely Son of your great Enemy.

JULIET

My onely Love sprung from my onely Hate:
Too early seen unknown, and known too late.
Prodigious Birth of Love it is to me.
That I must love a loathed Enemy.

ACT II

AS JULIET, RESTLESS AND UNABLE TO SLEEP, COMES OUT ON HER BALCONY AND THINKS OF ROMEO, HE SUDDENLY APPEARS BELOW HER IN THE GARDEN AND MAKES HIS WAY UP TO HER.

ROMEO

— But soft, what Light through yonder Window breaks?
It is the East, and Juliet is the Sun. . . .
The brightness of her Cheek would shame those Stars
As Day-light doth a Lamp; her Eyes in Heaven
Would through the Airy Region stream so bright
That Birds would sing and think it were not Night.
See how she leans her Cheek upon her Hand:
O that I were a Glove upon that Hand,
That I might touch that Cheek. . . .

JULIET

O Romeo, Romeo, wherefore art thou Romeo?
Deny thy Father and refuse thy Name;
Or if thou wilt not, be but sworn my Love
And I'll no longer be a Capulet.

JULIET

How camest thou hither, tell me, and wherefore?
The Orchard Walls are high and hard to climb,
And the place Death, considering who thou art,
If any of my Kinsmen find thee here.

ROMEO

With Love's light Wings did I o'erperch these Walls:
For Stony Limits cannot hold Love out,
And what Love can do, that dares Love attempt.
Therefore thy Kinsmen are no Stop to me.

JULIET

If they do see thee, they will murther thee.

ROMEO

Alack, there lies more Peril in thine Eye
Than twenty of their Swords; look thou but sweet,
And I am proof against their Enmity.

JULIET

I would not for the World they saw thee here.

ROMEO

I have Night's Cloak to hide me from their Eyes;
And but thou love me, let them find me here.
My Life were better ended by their Hate
Than Death prorogued wanting of thy Love.

THEY DANCE TOGETHER IN THE GARDEN AND ADMIT THEIR LOVE.

JULIET

Thou knowest the Mask of Night is on my Face,
Else would a Maiden Blush bepaint my Cheek
For that which thou hast heard me speak to night.
Fain would I dwell on Form; fain, fain deny
What I have spoke; but farewell, Complement.
Doest thou love me? I know thou wilt say 'I',
And I will take thy Word. Yet if thou swear'st,
Thou mayest prove false; at Lovers' Perjuries
They say Jove laughs. O gentle Romeo,
If thou dost love, pronounce it faithfully.
Or if thou thinkest I am too quickly won,
I'll frown and be perverse and say thee nay
So thou wilt woo; but else not for the World.
In truth, fair Mountague, I am too fond:
And therefore thou mayest think my 'Haviour light,
But trust me, Gentleman, I'll prove more true
Than those that have more Cunning to be Strange.
I should have been more Strange, I must confess,
But that thou overheard'st ere I was ware
My True-love Passion; therefore pardon me,
And not impute this yielding to Light Love
Which the Dark Night hath so discovered.

JULIET

My Bounty is as boundless as the Sea,
My Love as deep; the more I give to thee
The more I have, for both are infinite. . . .

ROMEO

O blessed, blessed Night. I am afeard,
Being in Night, all this is but a Dream,
Too flattering sweet to be substantial.

JULIET

Three Words, dear Romeo, and goodnight indeed.
If that thy bent of Love be honourable,
Thy purpose Marriage, send me Word to morrow,
By one that I'll procure to come to thee,
Where and what Time thou wilt perform the Right,
And all my Fortunes at thy Foot I'll lay
And follow thee my Lord throughout the World. . . .

ROMEO

How silver sweet sound Lovers' Tongues by Night,
Like softest Music to attending Ears. . . .
Let me stand here till thou remember it.

JULIET

I shall forget, to have thee still stand there,
Rememb'ring how I love thy Company.

ROMEO
And I'll still stay, to have thee still forget,
Forgetting any other Home but this.

JULIET
'Tis almost Morning: I would have thee gone,
And yet no farther than a Wanton's Bird,
That lets it hop a little from his Hand,
Like a poor Prisoner in his twisted Gyves,
And with a silken Thread plucks it back again,
So loving jealous of his Liberty.

ROMEO
I would I were thy Bird.

JULIET
Sweet, so would I;
Yet I should kill thee with much Cherishing.
Good night, good night: Parting is such sweet Sorrow
That I shall say good night till it be Morrow.

ROMEO

I'll tell thee ere thou ask it me again:
I have been feasting with mine Enemy,
Where on a sudden one hath wounded me
That's by me wounded; both our Remedies
Within thy Help and holy Physic lies.
I bear no Hatred, blessed Man: for lo,
My Intercession likewise steads my Foe. . . .
Then plainly know, my Heart's dear Love is set
On the fair Daughter of rich Capulet;
As mine on hers, so hers is set on mine,
And all combin'd save what thou must combine
By Holy Marriage. When and where and how
We met, we woo'd, and made exchange of Vow
I'll tell thee as we pass; but this I pray,
That thou consent to marry us to day.

ROMEO JOYFULLY EXECUTES A PASSÉ LEAP AFTER HE HAS RECEIVED A LETTER FROM JULIET IN WHICH SHE CONSENTS TO MARRY HIM . . .

...BUT THEY MUST DO SO IN SECRET.

FRIAR
So smile the Heavens upon this holy Act,
That After-hours with Sorrow chide us not.

ROMEO
Amen, amen. But come what Sorrow can,
It cannot countervail the exchange of Joy
That one short Minute gives me in her Sight.
Do thou but close our Hands with holy Words,
Then Love-devouring Death do what he dare.
It is enough I may but call her mine....
Ah Juliet, if the Measure of thy Joy
Be heap'd like mine, and that thy Skill be more
To blazon it, then sweeten with thy Breath
This neighbour Air, and let rich Music's Tongue
Unfold the imagin'd Happiness that both
Receive in either by this dear Encounter....

JULIET
But my true Love is grown to such Excess
I cannot sum up Sum of half my Wealth.

Friar Lawrence joins in holy matrimony the hands of the two kneeling lovers and hopes that their union will end, once and for all, the fighting between the Capulets and Mountagues.

ACT III

Tybalt tries to pick a fight with Romeo but Romeo will not fight with his wife's kinsman. Though Romeo begs him not to, Mercutio accepts the challenge. Tybalt stabs him and he dies, as a stunned, yet stoic Romeo looks on.

ROMEO
— Gentlemen, for Shame, forbear this Outrage. Tybalt, Mercutio: the Prince expressly hath Forbid this Bandying in Verona Streets. Hold, Tybalt, good Mercutio. . . .

MERCUTIO
I am hurt. A Plague a' both Houses: I am sped. . . .
A Plague a' both your Houses. They have made Worm's-meat of me. I have it, and soundly; to your Houses.

TO AVENGE MERCUTIO'S DEATH AND PRESERVE HIS FAMILY'S HONOUR, ROMEO ATTACKS TYBALT AND KILLS HIM.

ROMEO
— Now Tybalt, take the 'Villain' back again
That late thou gavest me: for Mercutio's Soul
Is but a little way above our Heads,
Staying for thine to keep him Company.
Either thou or I, or both, must go with him.

TYBALT
Thou wretched Boy that didst consort him here,
Shalt with him hence.

ROMEO
This shall determine that.

INNOCENTLY, JULIET WAITS FOR ROMEO ...

JULIET
Come Night, come Romeo, come thou Day in Night,
For thou wilt lie upon the Wings of Night
Whiter than new Snow upon a Raven's Back.
Come gentle Night, come loving, black-brow'd Night,
Give me my Romeo, and when I shall die,
Take him and cut him out in little Stars,
And he will make the Face of Heaven so fine
That all the World will be in love with Night
And pay no Worship to the garish Sun.
O I have bought the Mansion of a Love
But not possess'd it; and though I am sold,
Not yet enjoy'd. So tedious is this Day
As is the Night before some Festival
To an impatient Child that hath new Robes
And may not wear them.

...BUT IT IS HER NURSE WHO COMES TO HER WITH NEWS THAT MERCUTIO AND TYBALT ARE DEAD AND ROMEO HAS BEEN BANISHED FROM VERONA.

JULIET

Was woe enough if it had ended there;
Or if sower Woe delights in Fellowship,
And needly will be rank'd with other Griefs,
Why followed not, when she said 'Tybalt's dead',
'Thy Father' or 'thy Mother', nay, or both,
Which modern Lamentation might have mov'd,
But with a rearward following Tybalt's Death,
'Romeo is banished'. To speak that Word
Is Father, Mother, Tybalt, Romeo, Juliet,
All slain, all dead. Romeo is 'Banished':
There is no End, no Limit, Measure, Bound,
In that Word's Death, no Words can that Woe sound.

IN A SEQUENCE MORE POIGNANT BECAUSE OF THEIR IMPENDING SEPARATION, ROMEO KISSES JULIET IN HER BEDROOM AS THE SUN COMES IN THROUGH THE WINDOW, KNOWING THAT THEY MUST PART . . .

...THEIR EMBRACE MADE MORE POWERFUL BY THE FACT THAT NEITHER OF THEM KNOW WHEN THEY WILL BE ABLE TO HOLD EACH OTHER AGAIN.

JULIET
Wilt thou be gone? It is not yet near Day.
It was the Nightingale and not the Lark
That pierc'd the fearful Hollow of thine Ear...

ROMEO
It was the Lark, the Herald of the Morn,
No Nightingale. Look, Love, what envious Streaks
Do lace the severing Clouds in yonder East.
Night Candles are burnt out, and jocund Day
Stands tiptoe on the misty Mountaintops.
I must be gone and live, or stay and die.

JULIET
Yond Light is not Daylight, I know it, I:
It is some Meteor that the Sun exhales
To be to thee this Night a Torch-bearer
And light thee on thy way to Mantua.
Therefore stay yet, thou needst not to be gone.

ROMEO
Let me be ta'en; let me be put to death;
I am content, so thou wilt have it so.
I'll say yon Grey is not the Morning's Eye...
I have more care to stay than will to go:
— Come, Death, and welcome; Juliet wills it so.
— How is't, my Soul? Let's talk, it is not Day.

JULIET
It is, it is. Hie hence; be gone away.
It is the Lark that sings so out of Tune,...
O now be gone: more light and light it grows.

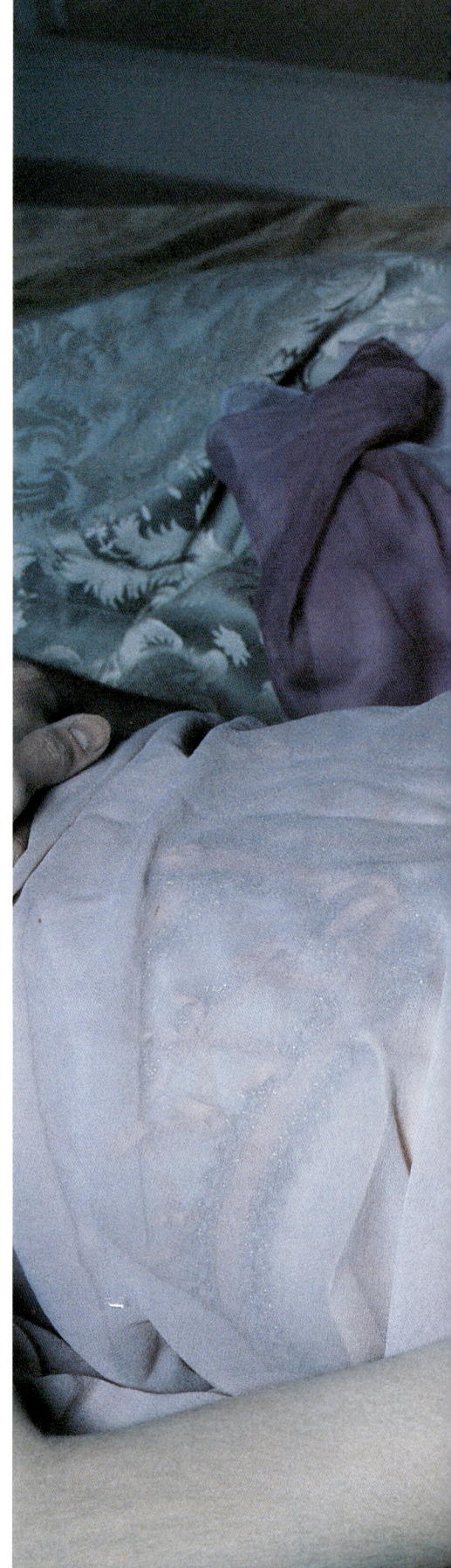

AFTER ROMEO LEAVES, JULIET'S FATHER ARRIVES WITH PARIS, WHO HE FEELS *IS* AN APPROPRIATE SUITOR, AND DESPITE JULIET'S IMPASSIONED PROTESTATIONS, HE INSISTS THAT SHE WILL MARRY PARIS COME THURSDAY AND ALLOW HIM TO COURT HER NOW.

JULIET
Good Father, I beseech you on my Knees,
Hear me with patience but to speak a Word.

CAPULET
hang thee, young Baggage, disobedient wretch.
I tell thee what: Get thee to Church a' Thursday,
Or never after look me in the Face.
Speak not, reply not, do not answer me.
My fingers itch. — Wife, we scarce thought us blest
That God had lent us but this onely Child;
But now I see this one is one too much,
And that we have a Curse in having her . . .

AS JULIET DANCES WITH PARIS, IT IS EVIDENT IN HER MOVEMENTS (ON POINT) THAT SHE DOES SO AGAINST HER WILL.

AFTER A FRANTIC INTERLUDE OF DESPERATE PRAYER, A DETERMINED JULIET RUSHES OFF TO SEE FRIAR LAWRENCE AND BEG FOR HIS HELP. HE WILL GIVE HER A VIAL OF SLEEPING POTION WHICH WILL INDUCE A DEATHLIKE TRANCE.

JULIET
I'll to the Friar to know his Remedy;
If all else fail, my self have power to die.

ACT IV

JULIET

— Come, Vial.
— What if this Mixture do not work at all?
Shall I be married then to morrow morning?
No, no, this shall forbid it. . . .
— Romeo, Romeo, Romeo, here's Drink: I drink to thee.

When her family comes to wake her, they find her "dead". And, in mourning, they move her to the family tomb.

ACT V

ROMEO

If I may trust the flattering Truth of Sleep,
My Dreams presage some joyful News at hand.
My Bosom's Lord sits lightly in his Throne,
And all this Day an unaccustom'd Spirit
Lifts me above the Ground with cheerful Thoughts.
I dreamt my Lady came and found me dead
(Strange Dream that gives a Dead-man leave to think)
And breath'd such Life with Kisses in my Lips
That I reviv'd and was an Emperor.
Ah me, how sweet is Love it self possess'd
When but Love's Shadows are so rich in Joy.

Romeo misinterprets a dream ("I dreamt my lady came and found me dead.... and breath'd such life with kisses in my lips that I revived") and thinks it a metaphor that presages their reunion, when, in reality, it was a portent of what was to come.

WHEN PARIS HAS SEEN ROMEO, DISGUISED AS A MONK, ATTEMPT TO OPEN JULIET'S TOMB, HE MISTAKENLY ASSUMES THAT ROMEO HAS COME TO DESECRATE HER BODY.... AS PARIS ATTACKS HIM, ROMEO THROWS OFF HIS CLOAK, A FIGHT BREAKS OUT AND PARIS IS KILLED. ... ROMEO ENTERS THE TOMB ALONE AND LIFTS JULIET FROM HER FUNEREAL BED AND DANCES WITH HER "DEAD" BODY IN HIS ARMS AS IF HE IS ATTEMPTING TO REVIVE HER BUT SHE FALLS LIMP AND LIFELESS.

ROMEO

— Ah dear Juliet,
Why art thou yet so Fair? I will believe, shall I believe,
That unsubstantial Death is amorous,
And that the lean, abhorred Monster keeps
Thee here in dark to be his Paramour?
For fear of that I still will stay with thee,
And never from this Pallet of dim Night
Depart again. Come lie thou in my arm:
Here's to thy Health, where e'er thou tumblest in.
Here, here will I remain,
With Worms that are thy Chambermaids; O here
Will I set up my everlasting Rest
And shake the Yoke of inauspicious Stars
From this World-wearied Flesh.— Eyes, look your last;
Arms, take your last Embrace; and Lips, O you
The Doors of Breath, seal with a righteous Kiss
A dateless Bargain to engrossing Death.
— Come, bitter Conduct; come unsavoury Guide.
Thou desperate Pilot, now at once run on
The dashing Rocks thy seasick, weary Bark.
Here's to my Love. O true Apothecary:
Thy Drugs are quick. Thus with a Kiss I die.

HE TAKES THE VIAL OF POISON HE HAS CONVINCED THE APOTHECARY TO SELL HIM ON LEARNING OF JULIET'S "DEATH" AND DRINKS.... JULIET WAKES AND FINDS ROMEO DEAD BESIDE HER AND HOPES THERE IS SOME POISON LEFT FOR HER.

JULIET

— What's here? A Cup clos'd in my True-love's Hand?
Poison I see hath been his timeless End.
— O Churl, drink all, and left no friendly Drop
To help me after. I will kiss thy Lips:
Haply some Poison yet doth hang on them
To make me die with a Restorative.
Thy Lips are warm.

ON FINDING NONE, SHE PICKS THE DAGGER UP FROM OFF THE FLOOR, PLUNGES IT INTO HER BREAST . . .

...AND TAKES HER PLACE AGAIN ON THE FUNERAL BIER, HER HANDS TOUCHING HIS LIGHTLY, JOINED FOREVER IN DEATH.

PRINCE
— Capulet, Mountague,
See what a Scourge is laid upon your Hate?
That Heaven finds means to kill your Joys with Love. . . .
A glooming Peace this Morning with it brings;
The Sun for Sorrow will not shew his Head.
Go hence to have more Talk of these Sad Things.
Some shall be pardon'd and some punished:
For never was a Story of more Woe
Than this of Juliet and her Romeo.